914·3

FOCUS ON

GERMANY

Albert W. L. McDonald

Evans Brothers Limited

For my Mother, Mary Wyllie Christie 1924-1991

Published by Evans Brothers Limited
2A Portman Mansions
Chiltern Street
London W1M 1LE

© Evans Brothers Limited 1992
Reprinted 1996 (twice)

Editor Caroline Sheldrick
Design by James Ralton
Map by Hardlines

Printed in Spain by GRAFO, S.A. – Bilbao

ISBN 0 237 51657 8

Acknowledgements
The author and publishers would like to thank the following for permission to reproduce the photographs: Bruce Coleman Limited – cover, 9 (top), 12 (left), David Davies, 18 (right) Thomas Bucholz, 21 (right), 22 Hans Reinhard Robert Harding Picture Library - contents page, 7, 11, 13 (left), 17 (right) Tony Waltham, 24 (left), 26, 29, 31 (left); Hutchison Picture Library -12 (right) Dave Brinicombe; Image Bank - 4 Keven Forest, 6 (left), 8, 9 (bottom) Daniel Hummel, 10 (left) Philip Kretchmar, 10 (right) Alan Becker, 13 (right), 15,16 (top) Michael Rosenfeld, (bottom) Peter Grumann, 17 (left), 18 (left) H.R. Uthoff, 19 (left), 23 Alain Choisnet, 24 (right) Benn Mitchell;Okapia Oxford Scientific Films - 20 (right top) Hans Dieter Brandl, (bottom right) W. Wisniewski, 21; Rex Features - title page, 14 Peter Stumpf, 27 (right) Adenis, 28(right),30 Travel Photo International-27(1eft);Zefa-6(right), 19(right), 25, 28 (left) K. Goebel, 31 (right) Dr Mueller.

Cover Magnificent Neuschwanstein Castle in Bavaria was built over 100 years ago as a wonderful mountain home by King Ludwig II of Bavaria. Ludwig wanted Neuschwanstein to be a beautiful fairy-tale palace to thrill and amuse his friends. He built quaint towers, rich hall and an underground grotto full of strange rock formations.

Title page Thinking about the past and looking forward to the future. Hundreds of thousands of people gather around the Brandenburg Gate (Brandenburger Tor) in Berlin to celebrate the reunification of Germany at midnight on October 3rd 1990.

Opposite Powerful barges from many countries carry freight and containers on Germany's mighty network of wide rivers and ship canals. One barge can carry as many containers as a fleet of 30 large lorries or push up to nine barges full of coal, grain, gravel or oil.

Contents

Introducing Germany

Hanging proudly outside Frankfurt am Main's ancient town hall, the new German flag unites the people of one of the largest countries in western Europe.

Germany is one of the youngest states in Europe. It was formed on October 3rd 1990 when the Federal Republic of Germany (FRG) and the German Democratic Republic (GDR) were re-united. Many hundreds of thousands of people, from both the FRG and the GDR, joined the unification party in the centre of Berlin.

As the crowds counted down the last few seconds to midnight, the new black, red and gold German flag was unfurled and fluttered in the cold night air. These celebrations were only the beginning of building a new state. The first elections to parliament, the Bundestag, were held in December 1990.

Unification has also brought many problems. It is taking time to replace old inefficient factories with modern industries and to create new jobs for the many thousands of people who are still unemployed. Germans are paying the costs of unification in higher taxes, higher prices, lower wages and greater unemployment.

Size and landscape

Germany is one of the largest countries in western Europe. It stretches over 900 kilometres from the sweeping sandy beaches of the North and the Baltic Seas, to the jagged peaks of the towering Alps. From the borders of Luxembourg and Belgium, in the west, Germany extends more than 640 kilometres eastwards to the River Oder and the frontier with Poland.

From north to south the landscape changes. The northern lowlands are an area of fertile farmland, bustling ports and unspoilt heathlands. Further south, in the central German uplands, there are rolling hills, industrial towns and deep wooded valleys. The southern German uplands are a mixture of dramatic hills, romantic forests, and ancient cathedral towns. The alpine foothills and Bayerische Alpen, in the deep south, have beautiful alpine meadows, pretty ski resorts and magnificent snow-capped mountains.

A hardworking people

Germany is already a very prosperous country. It has wide areas of fertile farmland, oil, gas and coal reserves. It has many modern industries and is one of the greatest trading nations in the world. Germans are a hardworking and determined people. They are keen that the problems of unification should be quickly solved.

DENMARK

North Sea

Baltic Sea

Nordfriesische Inseln

SCHLESWIG-HOLSTEIN

WATT

Helgoland

Ostfriesische Inseln

• Kiel

Rügen

• Rostock

MECKLENBURG-VORPOMMERN

• Lübeck
• Schwerin

HAMBURG

R. Elbe

NETHERLANDS

BREMEN

NIEDERSACHSEN

POLAND

• Lingen

HANNOVER

R. Weser

SACHSEN-ANHALT

BRANDENBURG

• BERLIN

R. Oder

Potsdam

• Magdeburg

• Münster

NORDRHEIN-

RUHR

WESTFALEN

HARZ

▲ Brocken
1142m

Cottbus

• Dortmund

• Halle

• Leipzig

• DÜSSELDORF

WESTERWALD

THÜRINGEN

SACHSEN

Dresden

BELGIUM

• Köln

• Erfurt

• Weimar

• Chemnitz

• Aachen

• BONN

HESSEN

ERZGEBIRGE

R. Rhein

CZECH REPUBLIC

EIFEL

Wiesbaden

FRANKFURT
AM MAIN

R. Main

BÖHMER WALD

R. Mosel

Mainz

RHEINLAND-

LUXEMBOURG

PFALZ

Würzburg

NÜRNBERG

SAARLAND

• Saarbrücken

BADEN-

WÜRTTEMBERG

SCHWÄBISCHE ALB

R. Donau

BAYERN

FRANCE

• STUTTGART

SCHWARZWALD

• MÜNCHEN

Freiburg

BAYERISCHE ALPEN

AUSTRIA

SWITZERLAND

▲ Zugspitze 2963m

LIECHTENSTEIN

0   100km

5

People

Shoppers crowd Hohe Strasse in the centre of the city of Köln.

More people live in Germany than in any other country in Europe. In the last 45 years the population of Germany has grown from 60 million to almost 80 million. In the 1950s most German families had four or five children. Kindergartens and schools were busy, crowded places with up to 40 children in one class.

Since 1960 families have become smaller. Now most German families only have two or three children. There are fewer children of school age and the population has almost stopped growing. People born in the baby-boom years are now in their forties.

By AD 2010 the baby-boom generation will retire from work. Germany will have a much older population. In years to come there will be many fewer than 80 million Germans.

Before reunification many stores in Halle's pedestrian precinct were run by the GDR government. There is now a growing number of privately run shops and a much greater choice of things to buy.

Migrating from east to west

Before unification many Germans left the GDR and moved west to look for work and to set up home in the old FRG. Some people went to join relatives in the west. Others hoped to find better jobs, to make more money and to live more comfortably than they could in the east. More than 350,000 people moved from the GDR, in the east, to the old FRG in the west, in late 1990.

In the same year another 750,000 migrants travelled through the GDR and into the old FRG from Poland, Romania, Czechoslovakia, Hungary, Bulgaria and what was then the USSR. For many it was the first time in more than 30 years that they were allowed to leave their home countries by their own governments. Families from the GDR towns of Schwerin, Weimar and Chemnitz migrated with only a few hours' preparation and taking only those belongings they could carry. Doctors left their hospitals, teachers their classrooms, and miners their pits. All hoped to benefit from the economic miracle which had made the old FRG one of the wealthiest countries in Europe.

Moving to the countryside

Most Germans still live in the towns and cities but many families have moved to the smaller villages in the countryside. New roads and faster rail services now allow people to live in the country and travel to work in town each day. Homes in the pretty rural villages can often cost much more than those in and round the towns and cities. Families who can afford to move into the countryside enjoy living in beautiful surroundings well away from traffic congestion and pollution from factories.

Immigrant children in Duisburg play in front of some of the city's derelict housing. Many people who migrate into Germany live in the poorer areas of cities until they can afford to buy or rent a home in a more pleasant area.

Who are the Germans?

The German people had spread throughout central Europe by Roman times. More than 1,000 years ago a great German empire was founded. Its boundaries were often changed by war. The first empire lasted until defeated by France and split into small states in 1815. A second empire began in 1871 and lasted until the end of the First World War in 1918. It was then replaced by a German Republic and later by a third empire. German territory expanded until the end of the Second World War when it was split and divided between several countries including the FRG and the GDR. Although so often divided by war and religion, Germans are united by a common language and culture.

Farming

Over two million Germans work on the land. There are many different types of farm. In Schleswig-Holstein and Niedersachsen, in the north-west, large mixed family farms of about 50 hectares produce wheat, barley, cattle, pigs and sheep. Further south, in Rheinland-Pfalz, tiny 5-hectare holdings produce grapes for wine. In the north-east of Germany very large collective farms produce potatoes, sugar-beet and oats. Around Berlin, small market gardens grow carrots, salad crops and strawberries.

Family farms

Many of Germany's mixed family farms are too small to make good profits. Farmers often cannot find enough money to invest in

Harvesting wheat in Baden-Württemberg. Farmers can make a good living once their land has been consolidated. Many invest some of this income in new farm machinery and in improving their homes.

new machinery or improvements. Often one farm may be made up of many small isolated fields spread over a wide area. Many farmers work in a town during the week and then tend their land at weekends.

These family farms are being improved by consolidation. Scattered holdings are being replaced by new, larger farms. Often new farm roads and even farmhouses are built at the same time. Larger, regular fields make it much easier to use modern tractors and combine harvesters. New types of crop, chemical fertilizers and pesticides allow farmers to produce much more food.

Germany's mixed farms are now producing more wheat, barley, sugar-beet, potatoes, maize and many other crops than they did before. Improving mixed farms has been so successful that Germany now exports increasing amounts of food.

Supporting smaller farms

Many of Germany's smaller farms are so unprofitable that their owners abandon them. If no one cultivates the land, it is left fallow, and becomes rough scrub. Weeds quickly spread to neighbouring fields.

The government has bought and improved many of these smaller farms. These are then let to new farmers for a low rent. Farming co-operatives have been formed to help smaller farmers sell their

Big, old farm buildings in the Schwarzwald once housed a family, their farm animals, tools, and crops after harvesting. Now many of these buildings have been converted into modern spacious homes, and families earn additional income by providing accommodation for tourists.

This patchwork of fields in Bayern are some of the most fertile in southern Germany. Grants from the EC have helped farmers to make this one of the richest farming areas in Europe.

crops for the best price. Many have been encouraged to offer tourist accommodation to increase their income.

Reorganizing collective farms

In the years before unification many of the larger farms in the east of Germany were collected together. They were made into giant collective farms. These were run by managers and often employed hundreds of people. In Mecklenburg-Vorpommern and Brandenburg, collective farms produced wheat, sugar-beet, maize, rye, potatoes and vegetables. It was very difficult to run these large farms well, and often they produced much less than they might have done.

Now these collective farms are being reorganized and the German government hopes that they will produce much more food. Managers and employees now earn more if they produce more. Farmers are paid higher prices if they grow better quality crops and if their goods are fresher when they reach market. Some very large collective farms may be split into family farms of between 100 and 200 hectares.

Food, beer and wine

Germans enjoy eating and drinking. Many have a light breakfast of bread, jam and coffee early in the morning, a mid-morning snack and then their main cooked meal at midday. Lunch tends to be filling, plain and wholesome. Green salads, boiled cabbage, potatoes, chicken, fried pork cutlets and stew are some of the most popular dishes. Most Germans have a cold supper early in the evening. Often it is made of fresh brown bread, different kinds of spicy *würst* sausages, pickled fish and bottled vegetables. Beer is often drunk with meals, and coffee taken afterwards.

On Sunday afternoons, or on a special visit to a café, families enjoy coffee and rich cakes with lots of fresh whipped cream.

Boiled potatoes and sauerkraut casserole with apple, onion and sausage is the type of food enjoyed by many German families for lunch.

Regional variety

Visitors to Germany many years ago found that every area had its own special foods and ways of cooking. Almost every village had its own recipe for bread, and a *würst* sausage from Halle was very different from one from Leipzig only 20 kilometres away. Now there are fewer regional variations, but people in the north of Germany still eat more fish than those in the south and those in the west still eat more meat.

Some local recipes are now popular in many areas. Dresden *stollen* is a spicy Christmas cake enjoyed in many countries. Even more famous are fried pats of minced beef which are known throughout the world as 'hamburgers' after the German city Hamburg, where they were first made.

Beer

Germans drink more beer than almost any other nation. The country has 2,000

Thousands of people sample beers in one of the many tents at the annual Oktoberfest in München. This festival is the largest of its kind in the world.

breweries. The Bayern state brewery was founded in AD1040 and there are many others more than 400 years old. Some of the biggest, including the Dortmunder Union in Dortmund, are in the large industrial towns in the north-west.

All German beer must be brewed to strict purity standards and may only be made from hops, yeast, malt, and fresh, clean water. Many beers, including Löwenbräu from München (Munich) and Beck's from Bremen, are exported to other countries.

Wine

Most Germans drink wine before or after meals in the same way as the English might drink sherry and port. They enjoy rich, sweet, white, perfumed wines with lots of flavour. Many of these wines are produced along the Rivers Mosel, Main and Rhein and in the south-west of the country. Some of Germany's very best wines are grown around the little village of Rüdesheim on the banks of the Rhein. Several of the vineyards have been owned by the same families for more than 600 years. Many new vineyards have been planted on the higher land on either side of the river. Wine from this area often has a very light, dry flavour. Much of it is turned into sparkling wine and some is made into brandy at the Asbach Distillery at Rüdesheim.

The gently sloping vineyards of Schloss Vollrads in the Rheingau produce some of Germany's finest wines. The estate has produced wine for almost 700 years.

Gewürztaler
delicious honey and almond biscuits

Ingredients

ground almonds (25 grams)
ground ginger (½ teaspoon)
plain flour (400 grams)
sugar (175 grams)
butter (125 grams)
candied peel (75 grams)
honey (125 grams)
baking powder (½ teaspoon)
milk (37 grams)
chocolate icing (175 grams)

Method

Mix together the almonds, ginger, flour and sugar. Rub the butter into the mixture. Stir in 25 grams of chopped peel and the honey. Dissolve the baking powder in the milk, add it to the mixture and make a smooth dough. Roll dough very thinly, cut into rounds and bake in a hot oven (180°C) for 10-15 minutes. Cool and decorate with icing and the remaining peel.

11

Energy

Germany's industrial success was based on rich seams of high-quality coal. Germany had vast reserves in Saarland, at Aachen near Köln, and the Ruhr in Nordrhein Westfalen. Many of these seams have now been used up. Germany has turned to new forms of fuel to provide its homes, factories and railways with electricity.

Strip mining brown coal

More than 350 million tonnes of brown coal are mined in Germany every year. It is used to heat homes and to generate electricity. Close to Leipzig and Cottbus brown coal is often found very close to the surface and is easy to mine.

First of all buildings and trees are cleared and then huge earth movers strip away soil. Massive excavators cut long, wide slices from the top of these exposed coal seams. The excavators make a deafening noise and they produce great billowing clouds of fine coal dust which covers everything in the area with a thick film of dark brown grime. Once the coal has been cut away all that remains are deep vast pits which quickly fill with dark, oily water. It takes many years to replace the topsoil and to landscape these areas so that pits can become wooded lakes.

Digging brown coal close to Köln is cutting a deep wide chasm in the north German landscape. Huge machines crush the coal and transfer it onto conveyor belts or into railway wagons alongside. Large excavators and diggers often work day and night to provide fuel for the country's many thermal power stations.

A family's supply of brown coal is left on the pavement outside their apartment in Limburg until they can store it inside. This type of coal is very smokey and does not produce a great deal of heat but many people in the east of the country still use it for heating their homes and as fuel in their cooking stoves.

Swiftly flowing mountain streams in Bayern are dammed to provide homes, offices and factories with a renewable source of electricity.

New forms of energy

Many parts of Germany have been explored for oil and gas. Wells around Kiel, Hamburg, Hannover and Lingen, close to the borders with The Netherlands, all produce oil which is made into petrol, heating fuel, and chemicals. Prospectors have also found natural gas in Germany. Wells in Brandenburg, Sachsen-Anhalt and Thüringen produce enough fuel each year to power several electricity generating stations.

Swiftly flowing rivers in the south of Germany generate hydro-electricity. Near Erfurt in Thüringen water from the River Saal is pumped overnight to above a dam on the hillside. Each morning the water is released and used to generate power as it runs back down to the river. On many smaller rivers in Baden-Württemberg, water has been led down long steps and generates electricity as it cascades from one level to the next.

Nuclear power

One-third of Germany's electricity is generated by nuclear power. There are more than 25 nuclear power stations providing electricity for homes, offices and factories. Many of the reactors are large and modern. One new plant, at Brokdorf in Niedersachsen, is one of the biggest in the world. Many other reactors are now too small or too old to be operated safely.

A large nuclear power plant at Lubmin, on the Baltic Sea, was built in the 1980s to a Soviet design. It was similar to the reactor at Chernobyl, in the Ukraine, which exploded after an accident in 1986. Lubmin has been shut down because many Germans thought it too dangerous. It will take many years to completely close the plant. The site will have to be carefully looked after for many thousands of years to come.

One of the country's nuclear power stations towers over farmland and provides power for the surrounding area.

Industry

Germany's heavy industries are still based on rich reserves of metal ores and minerals. Many industries developed in the 1850s and, as they grew, Germany changed from a collection of small states into a mighty industrial empire. In the late 1930s Germany produced more iron, steel, ships, railway locomotives, steam engines and industrial machinery than any other nation.

The German economic miracle
In 1945 Germany was defeated in war. It lost ports, mines and large areas of land to the USSR and Poland. What remained was split into the FRG and GDR. Great cities lay in ruins, ports and railways were tangles of twisted metal and many of the nation's greatest industries were devastated.

In the following 40 years, leading to Germany's unification, many factories were rebuilt and new ones created. Germany's hard work created an economic miracle in the old FRG. Many of these industries are the most modern in Europe. Large chemical refineries, steel plants, engineering works and car factories have made Germany one of the world's wealthiest and most powerful nations. However, many Germans must now work much harder to compete with the new 'Tiger' economies of Japan, Korea and Malaysia.

Before reunification many of the chemical plants at Weimar, in the east of the country, pumped dangerous gases into the atmosphere. Now many of these have been closed and others have reduced their emissions.

Designing better cars
More than 4 million cars and minibuses are built in Germany every year. BMW, Audi, Volkswagen, Mercedes-Benz, and Porsche are all German companies. Ford and Vauxhall also have factories there. German factories manufacture some of the most advanced cars in the world. Many BMWs

have on-board computers; Audi have invented a steering wheel which moves safely out of the way to protect drivers in an accident; they have designed a recyclable car. Porsche, who manufacture sports cars near Stuttgart, fit every one with catalytic converters to alter harmful exhaust fumes. Germany now builds more cars than any other country in Europe.

Many of the people who build BMW's most expensive sports cars are part-time farmers who look after their crops in the evenings and at weekends.

New hi-tech products

When Germany was unified in 1990, many of the factories and businesses in the east were making a loss and so most of them were closed. More than one million people lost their jobs or only had work for two or three days each week. Since then many people from the east have found jobs in the west. Some travel great distances each day, others have moved house to be closer to their jobs. Many work making high-technology electrical equipment for companies such as Rowenta and Bosch. They both make kitchen appliances. Other factories make microchips, quartz watches, CDs and computers.

Technicians wearing protective clothing working in one of the country's most modern and advanced factories which produces microchips.

The Ruhr

The Ruhr region in Nordrhein-Westfalen has one of the greatest concentrations of industry in the world. High quality coal, iron, steel and chemicals are produced there. The Ruhr was at the centre of the German economic miracle which made the old FRG one of the wealthiest countries in Europe. Since 1960 many new factories have opened and cars, plastics, papers, textiles, clothing and much more is now made there. The Ruhr cities of Essen, Dortmund and Düsseldorf are some of the largest in Germany. Many of their factories make goods for export and others make components for Germany's many car plants.

Transport

Germany is at the very heart of Europe. The goods from many countries must pass through it on their way to market. Greek olive oil, Bulgarian wine, Norwegian timber, Italian furniture, Swiss watches and Spanish oranges – they all travel on German roads, railways or canals. Containers of machinery from as far away as Japan arrive after a journey from the Pacific along the trans-Siberian railway and through Poland.

Fast new autobahns

Germany is criss-crossed by a network of wide autobahns and has more kilometres of these fast motorways than any other European country. They have been built so that cars, buses and lorries can travel from one city to another as fast and as safely as possible. There is no speed limit on the autobahns. It can take as little as twelve hours to drive from Freiburg, in the south-west, to the island of Rügen, off the north-west coast.

Important autobahns link the capital Berlin, with the large cities of Rostock, Hamburg, Hannover, München and Dresden. Many new roads are now being built between the east and west sides of the country and more are planned.

High speed ICE trains

There are two different rail systems in Germany. Separate railways in the east and

Busy German autobahns are at the centre of Europe's growing motorway network. Now that many more people are free to travel from eastern Europe many existing roads are crowded at peak times.

Many railway engines and carriages in the GDR, like these in Leipzig station, were old and worn out. Germans are working hard to improve their rail service and to build new modern trains.

New Inter City Express trains (ICE) are amongst the fastest and most modern in Europe. They have been built by some of the most important engineering companies in Germany.

west of the country use different types of locomotive, goods wagon, and passenger coach. Both have very different safety and signalling systems and so it is very difficult to join them together. In the west of Germany modern railways can carry trains at up to 300 kilometres per hour.

A new fast inter-city express service (using ICE trains) began in 1990. These use both railway systems and link main cities all over Germany. ICE trains give a fast, efficient service between city centres. It is often quicker and easier to use an ICE train than to fly. Additional trains are added to the timetables on important holidays and in the summer.

The crossroads of Europe
Many of Germany's rivers have been made deeper and wider so that they can carry large ships. Ocean-going vessels move cargoes of coal, ore, steel, machinery and chemicals from North Sea ports to Germany's southern border with Switzerland. Powerful tugs pull large barges roped together on the Rhein. Each barge can carry 1,000 tonnes of cargo and one tug can push nine together. The River Rhein is a super highway for ships. By the riverside city of Köln, large vessels pass up and down the Rhein every minute of the day and night.

Germany's river system has been extended by building canals. Ships on the mighty Mittlelland Canal can sail all the way across the country from The Netherlands to Poland. In Bayern, the Main-Donau canal links the Rhein with Austria, Hungary, Serbia, Romania, Bulgaria and the Black Sea. Other canals join the country to France Luxembourg, Belgium and The Netherlands.

A powerful freight barge from Petershagen passes another on a busy canal linking Germany with The Netherlands. Many of the country's canals are wide super highways which link the North Sea with the Black Sea, and the Baltic with the Mediterranean.

Northern coasts

Holiday villages, quiet sandy beaches, lonely lighthouses and busy ports are just some of the different things that visitors find on Germany's northern coasts and islands.

Beach holidays

Many families enjoy beach holidays on the Baltic and North Sea shores. All along the Mecklenburg-Vorpommern coast, villages and towns are crowded with tourists every summer. Germans like to bathe in the sea and so hotels, holiday villages and camp sites are always close to beaches. During late June, July and August the safe, shallow waters of the Baltic are full of people swimming, sailing and windsurfing.

Sandy beaches and dunes stretch for 40 kilometres on Sylt, one of the Nordfriesische islands, off the North Sea coast. Many Germans spend holidays there each year. Visitors to the tiny North Sea island of Heligoland can enjoy fresh seafood from the only lobster fishery in Germany.

Lübeck

For many hundreds of years Lübeck was one of the richest and most powerful ports in northern Europe. Some of this great wealth was used to build one of the finest cities in Germany. The old town lies between the river and the canal, and is

Colourful wicker chairs dot a popular tourist beach in Schleswig-Holstein. Many German families enjoy an annual holiday at the seaside and create a small private space on the beach by building little sand walls around their chairs.

Lübeck's mighty city gate, the Holstentor, was built in 1477. It was badly damaged by war earlier this century but has now been rebuilt and restored.

nearly surrounded by water. It has many beautiful buildings, some over 500 years old. Many of these ancient houses, churches and port buildings are being carefully preserved and restored.

Changing the coast

Large power stations, shipyards and oil refineries have changed Germany's coasts. These huge buildings are seen from many kilometres away. Often the sea and the beaches around them are very dirty. Birds, seals and fish are endangered and tourists stay away. Many Germans want their coasts to be protected and now it is very difficult to build there.

Stralsund, on the Baltic coast, is a busy port-city which has kept many of its charming old buildings. It is an ancient city but now has many new industries.

Hamburg

Hamburg is the second largest city in Germany and the country's busiest port. Its harbour is full of merchant ships from all over the world. Smaller vessels come and go from the port along Germany's network of rivers and canals. Hamburg has large shipyards, chemical works and machinery factories. Much of Hamburg has been rebuilt since 1950 and today it is an attractive modern city. It has a popular opera house and a music hall. Many people from all over north Germany visit the city's shops, sports arenas and theatres.

Hamburg's commercial docks are crowded by large containers being unloaded from large ocean-going freighters. Many of these will be carried far inland and to neighbouring countries on smaller river barges.

Rügen

Rügen is the largest and one of the most beautiful German islands. It has tall beech woods, towering white cliffs, broad bays and an important nature reserve. Many thousands of holidaymakers and tourists now visit the island every year. Many people are attracted by its unspoilt environment and peaceful atmosphere but as more and more people visit the island its beaches become more crowded, its roads busier and its woods noisier. Too many people can often spoil the environment of beautiful remote places like Rügen.

Conservation

From the windswept island of Rügen, on the Baltic coast, to the pine forests of the Böhmer Wald, on the frontiers of Austria, many naturally beautiful areas of Germany are endangered by industry. Many places are now protected and Germans are trying to restore and protect others.

Protecting the Watt

The area of mud flats and sandbanks called the Watt, on Germany's North Sea coast, are the home of crabs, grey seals, and many different seabirds. The Watt is one of the natural wonders of Europe. Even a spoonful of its sea water may contain one million microscopic creatures. At low tide these coastal mud flats stretch up to 16 kilometres from the coast, and are crowded by tiny crabs sieving food from the rich oozing mud.

The Watt is in danger from growing numbers of tourists, factories on the coast and from chemicals brought down from industrial areas by the Rivers Weser and Elbe.

Germans cherish their coasts and so this wide breathtaking area is now one of the largest bird reserves in Europe. Gulls, terns and avocets are protected and allowed to rear their young in peace. The building of factories and tourist homes has been halted in many places and Germany has new strict laws to ensure that rivers are cleaner.

A group of visitors in a horse-drawn cart enjoy the isolation and natural beauty of the Watten Meer National Park.

In the past, nesting birds have been disturbed and seals have been poisoned but now the Watt is a protected area and one of the largest bird reserves in Europe.

Clearings carpeted in glowing heather help to make the Lüneburg Heath one of the most attractive natural areas in Germany.

Preserving the Lüneburg Heath

The Lüneburg Heath is an ancient landscape of small farms, forests, heath and bog. Thousands of years ago it was part of a great oak forest which stretched from France to Russia. Over many hundreds of years clearings were made and these now give this beautiful area its name and character. In autumn the Heath is a great expanse of pink and purple heather. It is the home of roe and fallow deer, pheasants, black cocks, and large cranes. Many people visit the Heath every year to enjoy the unspoilt countryside.

Great flocks of sheep used to roam the area and kept the heathlands open by grazing on the shoots of new trees. Now fewer sheep are kept, and trees are again invading clearings. The Lüneburg Heath is in danger of changing back to forest. Conservation volunteers visit the Heath every spring and remove tree shoots. They aim to preserve the landscape as it has been for centuries.

Cleaner air

Once the air around many of the large factories in Germany was polluted. Smoke from the chimneys of chemical plants in Leipzig, steel works at Magdeburg and heavy industry close to Berlin darkened skies all around. Great smog clouds of smoke and dangerous chemicals hung over many large industrial cities. Smog could make people very ill and also damage the brick and stonework of buildings.

Germans want their country to be a clean and pleasant place in which to live. Many of the oldest and most dirty factories were closed down in the early 1990s. Others have taken great care to reduce the amount of smoke, dust and chemical pollution that they produce. New laws have been passed to limit the amount of exhaust fumes that can be produced by cars, buses and lorries. The air above many cities is now fresher and cleaner than it has been for years.

A thick smog of car exhaust fumes and smoke from factories hangs in the air above Frankfurt am Main. The air quality in Germany is often very poor, but new laws have recently been passed to improve the environment.

Forests and mountains

Deep in the centre of Germany lies all that is left of a dark mysterious forest. Once, many hundreds of years ago, forest covered the whole country. It was cut down for building timber, fuel and to make way for fields. Between 1750 and 1850 German forests were replanted, and now they cover one-third of the country.

New forests

Germany is one of the most wooded lands in Europe. Trees cover large areas in the east, where they are grown as a crop and are harvested every 30 years. Well-managed woods cover the rolling hills of Thüringen and Hessen. Spruce trees give these uplands a wild, romantic look. They are cover for pheasants, black cock and deer on large hunting estates. The forests are the home of racoons, otters, mink, wildcats and foxes. They also provide Germany with a valuable supply of timber for industry.

The south of the country is a patchwork of woods and fields. Farmers in Bayern often have more than half of their farms planted with tall fir trees. Thick, dark pine forests clothe the lower slopes of the Bayerische Alpen and are the home of the rare lynx. Trees grow up the mountain sides until it is too high and too cold for them to survive.

Germans are very concerned that many of these forests are being badly damaged by

Pine trees in the Schanwald, their tops broken and their trunks stripped of bark, are slowly being killed by acid rain. Many trees which have taken a century to grow have been destroyed by pollution in only a few years.

industrial pollution. The chimneys of older power stations, burning brown coal, release dangerous gases. These can make rain acid.

Acid rain can damage and kill trees. Forests in south Germany and on the borders with the Czech Republic have been harmed. The scorched tops of trees show that many are dying. Now Germany is asking neighbouring countries to reduce these emissions of harmful gases.

22

Fairy-tales and superstitions

Romantic forests, ancient villages, fairy-tale castles and towering mountains are at the heart of most German myths. Witches, gnomes, werewolves and vampires have all been said to haunt mysterious woods. Silver miners in the Harz mountains used to tell of wicked *wichtlein* who lived in the mines. These tiny goblins stole tools, blew out candles and played all sorts of cruel tricks. Legend has it that giant spectres, or ghosts, stalk the summit of the Brocken, the highest mountain in central Germany. Even today, in certain lights, climbers report seeing gigantic misty figures walk across the clouds, waving to onlookers.

Spas and ski resorts

Dramatic snow-covered alpine peaks rise high above the forests and divide Germany from Switzerland and Austria. Clear mountain springs gush from the rocks of their foothills. Many Germans visit these mountain springs to drink the mineral water. In some places, where the water is sparkling and warm, it is used to fill the bathing pools of health resorts.

Higher in the Bayerische Alpen are the best ski resorts in Germany. Many have

snow for three months each year and some villages have ice rinks, ski jumps and bob-sleigh runs. Mountain railways carry tourists up to the higher slopes where there is sometimes enough snow to ski in summer. Cable-cars reach the highest peaks. From the summit of the Zugspitze, the highest mountain in Germany, there are spectacular views. One can see deep gorges, glacial lakes and jagged snow-covered mountain ridges.

Visitors to the lookout point at Garmisch Partenkirchen enjoy one of the most spectacular mountain views in Germany. Mountain railways and winter sports facilities make this one of the most popular tourist resorts in Bavaria.

Soon after reunification Germany issued a new stamp to celebrate the World Masters Bobsleigh Championships at Altenberg. In the past the GDR Olympic teams trained on Altenberg's steep and winding run.

Schwarzwald
The Black Forest

This beautiful area of forests, farmland and mountains is one of the most popular holiday areas in Europe. In the valleys there are ancient, half-timbered spa villages with pretty little churches. Traditional inns and posthouses offer visitors a friendly welcome. Dark, brooding pine forests on the hills above give the area its name. Titsee Lake, surrounded by thick, wild forests and romantic hills, is one of the most attractive places in Germany. Todtnau, where the world-famous 'Snowshoe Club' was founded in 1891, is one of the oldest skiing resorts in Europe.

Villages and towns

Germans take great pride in their neat villages and well-ordered towns. Often these have grown up over hundreds of years but, because of war damage, many have been rebuilt. Beautiful old houses, churches and palaces have been carefully restored and bright modern homes, shops, schools and offices have been built alongside.

Dresden's magnificent churches and palaces were some of the most beautiful in the world before they were damaged by war earlier this century.

Village life

Villages are pleasant places to live and houses are often well built and cared for. Homes are usually very comfortable with double or triple glazing, central heating and rolling steel shutters which keep rooms cool in summer and warm in winter. Churches are at the centre of village life and often their halls are busy with clubs, meetings and music every afternoon and evening.

Germans like to buy fruit and vegetables as fresh as possible and so even small villages have small open markets where local farmers sell potatoes, carrots, cabbages, apples and grapes. Most villages have kindergartens, where children begin school at three years of age, and *grundschules* for children from six to nine years old.

Travelling to work

Many of the people who live in villages work in shops, offices and factories in nearby towns. In Bayern many people leave their homes before dawn to drive north, from small lakeside villages, to work in the large modern BMW factory at München. When they arrive home from work, early in the afternoon, many tend tiny vineyards, work small farms or run decorating and building businesses from home.

Many vegetables in München's colourful market are grown by local farmers and on smallholdings around the city.

The ancient Wartburg castle, towering 200 metres above the town of Eisenach, became a popular tourist site after reunification.

A town in Thüringen

Eisenach was founded over 800 years ago and is one of the oldest towns in Germany. It has an ancient castle, historic churches and many beautiful old houses. Until 1990 it was in the old GDR, and many of the town's 45,000 people lost their jobs when Eisenach's older factories closed after unification. At first many families left the town, but now it is a busy bustling place full of newly-built hotels, smart shops and bright, modern factories.

There are new autobahns and the local railways were improved. A big factory was built by Bosch to make washing machines and dishwashers. BMW and Opel both built car plants. Now many people in Eisenach have well-paid jobs and many feel better off than ever before. There are many more small shops in the town and a much larger choice of foods, clothes and furniture. It was difficult for people in the GDR to buy foreign cars but since unification many families in Eisenach have sold their old GDR-made Trabants and bought Volkswagens, Opels and BMWs.

Eisenach is an historic town and, since unification, it has become a popular place for tourists from as far away as Japan and America. It was in Eisenach in 1521 that Martin Luther translated the Bible into German. Johann S. Bach, the famous composer, was born there in 1685. People travelling by car along the 'Castle and Thüringen' tourist road pass through the town, and Eisenach is the starting point for a long distance hiking trail. Many people in Eisenach now look after tourists and work in hotels, restaurants and shops.

Nürnberg Christkindlmarkt

Stalls selling Christmas decorations, spicy ginger cakes and pretty presents crowd the streets in the centre of Nürnberg in the weeks before Christmas. The sounds of carol singers and brass bands fill the air, clowns and street entertainers amuse shoppers and everywhere there is the feeling of fun and expectation. Many thousands of people from all over Germany visit the market every year. Shoppers crowd the streets from early in the morning until well after dark. Late in the evening stalls are lit by lanterns, candles and fairylights as visitors to the city buy carved cuckoo clocks, beautiful dolls and hand-made wooden toys.

Berlin

This stamp celebrating German unity was issued on the 3rd of October, 1990.

Berlin is one of the most exciting and interesting capital cities in Europe. Its shopping streets are busy with people from all over the world and pavements are crowded with stalls selling handcrafts, posters and badges. City nightclubs offer a magical mix of music, entertainment and dancing. The whole city has an atmosphere of fun and the unexpected.

Wir sind ein Volk

Berlin was reunited after 30 years when the first blocks of a massive border wall were broken down on November 9th 1989. Thousands of people cheered and television cameras sent live pictures around the world. Until then, West Berlin was an isolated island of FRG territory in the middle of the GDR.

West Berlin was divided from the east of the city and from the countryside all around by a massive wall, barbed wire and tall lookout towers. People trying to cross into West Berlin without permission were shot by GDR border guards.

The Berlin Wall divided families, cut through villages and split farms in two. Once it was opened hundreds of thousands of people flooded through. The east and west sides of the city were reunited for the first time since 1961. Germans from the two sides embraced, cheered and sang 'Wir sind ein Volk', 'We are one people'.

The Kufurstendam area of central Berlin at night is one of the most exciting streets in Europe. The pavement cafés, cinemas, nightclubs and street markets are crowded until late into the night.

Around Alexanderplatz, in the heart of what was East Berlin, many Germans shop for cheap food and inexpensive clothing. The Markethall is a maze of tiny crowded stalls selling local produce and imported items.

Germany's capital

Berlin became the capital city when Germany was unified on October 3rd 1990. The Bundestag, Germany's parliament, meets in the city and it has many new government offices. Berlin is an ancient city and earlier this century it was the capital of a vast empire known as the Deutsch Reich. It still has a magnificent parliament building and wide avenues lined by large imposing old ministries.

Germans are working hard to make Berlin into a modern capital for their country. Old buildings are being made into bright new government offices with hi-tech equipment. Many countries are opening new embassies and German civil servants are moving to the city from the old FGR capital at Bonn. Roads linking the city with the rest of Germany are being improved.

Once one of the main stores in East Germany, Alex in Alexanderplaz is now one of the largest shops in Berlin. It was one of the first inefficient industries to be sold after reunification.

Rebuilding Berlin

New homes, offices and shops are being built all over Berlin. A new exciting city centre is being created to replace one destroyed by war in the 1940s. It will cover a vast area in the middle of the new capital and already there are plans for new shopping malls, hotels, cinemas and theatres. Berlin's cathedral, historic buildings and great monuments now proudly stand in the middle of the emerging new city centre.

Brilliantly floodlit, surrounded by a vast sea of people and crowned by exploding fireworks, the Brandenburger Tor was at the centre of the celebrations of German reunification.

The heart of the nation

The great arch of the Brandenburger Tor was built in 1791 to celebrate a great German victory and is one of Berlin's oldest monuments. The first parts of the Berlin Wall to be broken open in 1989 were in front of the arch. Germans see the Brandenburger Tor as a symbol of their unity, and Berlin as the political and cultural heart of the German nation.

Culture and customs

Germans are a very cultured people who enjoy literature and the arts. Every town of any size has its own theatre and many have their own orchestras. Germans have written much of the world's most popular classical music. Many great operas are also by German composers. Millions of foreign tourists visit the country's festivals every year.

Writers

The works of many German writers are well known throughout the world. Karl Marx, the father of communism, and Martin Luther, the protestant reformer, have both changed the course of history. Others have written fascinating stories and poems.

Johann von Goethe is one of the country's greatest writers. He was born in Frankfurt am Main in 1749 and died at Weimar when he was 82 years old. His most famous play was about sad Dr Faust who made a pact with a terrible devil. At first many of the Doctor's wishes were granted but in the end he was dragged down to hell.

Johann von Schiller was a close friend of Goethe. He was a professor and one of Germany's best-known poets. He wrote about William Tell, a Swiss farmer who fought to defend his country when it was invaded. This story is famous throughout Europe.

Dresden's Semper house was build in 1879 and is one of the most beautiful buildings in the country. It is a popular place for German families and tourists to spend an evening.

Villagers in the tiny mountain village of Oberammergau act out a scene from the Last Supper showing Jesus Christ and His disciples. The play has been performed every ten years since 1643.

28

Music

Germans love listening to classical music. They have over 100 orchestras, whose conductors can choose from a wide range of German music. Telemann, Bach, Handel, Gluck, Haydn, Mozart, Beethoven, Wagner, Schoenberg and Hindemith are just a few of the most famous German composers whose music is played throughout the world.

Germany's great cathedral churches hold festivals of magnificent organ music. People from all over the world travel to the tiny mountain village of Oberammergau, in Bayern, to see the passion play. It tells the story of the last days of Jesus Christ.

Every village of any size has its own brass band or folk group and many people enjoy playing jazz and popular music.

Playing out the story of the Pied Piper of Hameln, an actor and some children dance through the streets of Hameln. Legend tells of how a mysterious Piper led a great plague of rats from the town many hundreds of years ago and then returned to take the town's children when the Mayor and Councillors refused to pay his fee.

Festivals

Cheerful carnivals and great festivals are popular all over Germany. People like celebrations. On warm summer afternoons the pretty little village of Hameln, near Hannover, is crowded as a Pied Piper leads children around the streets. The Lake Night Festival at Konstanz, in Baden-Württemberg, ends with a gigantic firework display. People in the Harz mountains welcome the month of May with lively parties and great bonfires. In August the Rhein is aflame with illuminations for many kilometres south of Koblenz. Throughout the year there are fancy dress parades, folk dances, pageants, processions and great cavalcades of riders on horseback held all over the country.

Many festivals are held during the main religious holidays. Carnivals take place in Köln, Aachen, Mainz and München on Shrovetide at the beginning of Lent and a great passion play is held at Rothenburg ob der Tauber at Whitsun.

Jacob and Wilhelm Grimm

One hundred and fifty years ago, these two brothers collected tales of peasants, princes, dwarfs, giants and fairies from all over Germany. They were well educated men and both were professors in Berlin. Their fairy stories delighted both children and adults of the time. Since then, their tales of Hansel and Gretel, and of Rumpelstiltskin, have been printed in many different languages. The story of an ugly frog, who was freed from the spell of a wicked witch and transformed into a handsome prince by a beautiful princess, is told as a bedtime story all over the world.

Germany and the world

Germany is one of the most successful trading nations in the world and it is the largest and most powerful country in the European Union. Germans want to live and work at the centre of a peaceful, prosperous Europe. Their industries try hard to compete against those of Britain, France, the USA, Japan and Korea. Their success gives them one of the world's highest standards of living. Germans enjoy more holidays abroad than any other nation in Europe.

The hub of Europe

Germany exports and sells more cars, televisions, video recorders, fridges, freezers and many other manufactured goods than any other European country. It is at the centre of a free trade area covering the countries of western Europe and Scandinavia. German companies can sell their goods just as easily in Austria, Finland or Portugal as they can in Germany itself.

Germans are keen to work closely with neighbouring countries and to make Europe a better place to live. They sent long convoys of trucks carrying food aid to the Soviet Commonwealth when the harvest there failed. They delivered free electricity to Romania when its dangerous power stations were closed.

Germans invested heavily in the industries of eastern European countries. In 1990, the German car makers Volkswagen bought most of the Skoda car factory in Czechoslovakia.

The Skoda car plant at Mladaboleshad now produces more advanced cars with the help of the German car makers Volkswagen. Many other German companies have invested money, skills and know-how in factories in neighbouring countries of eastern Europe.

Hannover's international trade fair attracts business people and buyers from all over the world. German companies exhibit at the fair to show their best, most modern and most advanced products.

Selling cars abroad

Most German cars are well designed, expertly built and have a high reputation in other countries. Porsche, BMW and Mercedes-Benz all make high quality, luxury cars for sale throughout the world. Many people abroad look on more expensive German cars as a status symbol.

Many countries can now produce less expensive cars than Germany. Many German car factories have become smaller over the last few years and less cars are being produced. Many companies now design and build expensive high quality cars to compete on the world market. German cars even sell well in those foreign countries which have their own car factories.

Germans on holiday

Germans enjoy going on holiday and they love travelling to other countries. Many families spend two weeks in the summer exploring the mountains of Norway, enjoying sunshine and water sports around the Mediterranean or flying off to distant tropical islands. In winter many families spend a week skiing in France, Italy, Switzerland or Austria. Germans have a great sense of adventure and many also visit the USA, India, China and Africa.

Germans are prosperous tourists, and most countries welcome the money that they spend while on holiday. The Deutsch Mark is one of the world's most popular currencies.

The Reichstag, in the centre of Berlin, is an imposing old building which is again the home of Germany's parliament. It was built a century ago but much of the interior is new and modern.

Index and summary

Area:	356,945 square kilometres
Population:	80 million (20% rural; 80% urban)
Bordering:	Netherlands, Belgium, Luxernbourg, France, Switzerland, Austria, Czechoslovakia, Poland and Denmark
Capital:	Berlin
Main cities:	Hamburg, München, Köln, Essen, Frankfurt am Main, Dortmund, Düsseldorf, Stuttgart, Leipzig, Bremen, Duisburg, Hannover, Dresden, Nurnberg Magdeburg, Wiesbaden, Kiel, Erfurt, Saarbrücken Mainz, Potsdam and Schwerin
States:	Baden-Wurttemberg, Bayern, Berlin, Brandenburg, Bremen, Hamburg, Hessen, Mecklenburg Vorpornrnem, Niedersachsen, Nordrhein-Westfalen, Rheinland-Pfalz, Saarland, Sachsen, Sachsen-Anhalt, Schleswig-Holstein, and Thüringen
Language:	German
Religion:	Protestant (69%), Roman Catholic (9%)
Main industries:	Iron, steel, transportation equipment, machinery and chemicals
Main crops:	Sugar-beet, potatoes, wheat, barley
Forest area:	103,000 square kilometres (29% of total area)
Currency:	100 Pfennigs to 1 Deutsch Mark
National airline:	Lufthansa
Longest river:	Rhein
Highest point:	Zugspitze, 2,963 metres